EIGHTH NOTE PUBLICATIONS

Reverie

Ryan Meeboer

Reverie is a lyrical piece reflecting someone in a dream-like state. It is a peaceful song using repetitive melodic figures, lush harmonies, and simple rhythms.

As with all lyrical piece, balance is key. The chorale-like style is important to establish the beauty and peacefulness of the piece.

When working through this piece, it is important to focus on strong air support and gentle articulations, allowing players to perform rhythmic figures without changing the legato effect of the piece.

Dynamic swells, such as those in the opening measures, can be performed with as much dramatic effect as the ensemble chooses; just be sure that any melodic material can be heard.

Finally, after the piece thins out at measure 39, be sure that measure 43 isn't too overpowering when the trombone/tuba enters. Try to make it gentle, yet dramatic, building into the final measures of the piece.

Ryan Meeboer is a music educator, who obtained his degree through the Ontario Institute for Studies in Education at the University of Toronto. As a composer, he has written and arranged many pieces for concert band, jazz band, and small ensembles. His young band piece, *Last Voyage of the Queen Anne's Revenge*, has been well received by performers, educators, and audiences, and his pieces are starting to be found on festival and contest lists. As a performer, he has had experience in several groups, including concert and stage bands, chamber choir, vocal jazz ensemble, acoustic duets, and the Hamilton based swing group, "The Main Swing Connection".

Ryan began studying music at the age of seven through private guitar lessons. During his years in elementary and secondary school, he gained experience in several families of instruments. Focusing on music education and theory (including composition and orchestration), he attended McMaster University to achieve his honours degree in music. Ryan is currently a teacher for the Halton District School Board in Ontario, where he continues to compose and arrange.

Please contact the composer if you require any further information about this piece
or his availability for commissioning new works and appearances.

ryan.meeboer@enpmusic.com

ISBN: 9781771578073
CATALOG NUMBER: BQ221528
COST: $15.00
DURATION: 3:00
DIFFICULTY RATING: Easy
Brass Quintet

www.enpmusic.com

REVERIE

Ryan Meeboer

REVERIE

B♭ Trumpet 1

Ryan Meeboer

REVERIE

Bb Trumpet 2

Ryan Meeboer

F Horn

REVERIE

Ryan Meeboer

Trombone

REVERIE

Ryan Meeboer

Tuba

REVERIE

Ryan Meeboer

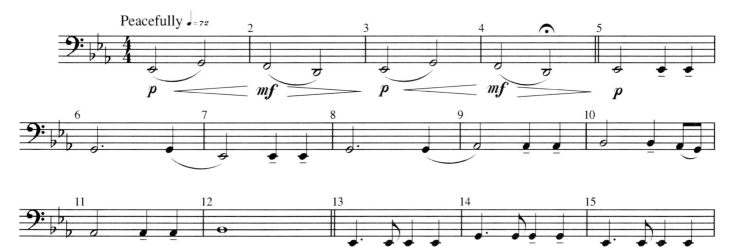

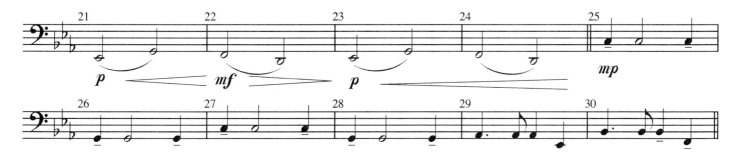

REVERIE pg. 2